Why Can't I Fly?

D0746308

For Ruth

Copyright © 1990 by Ken Brown

All rights reserved. No reproduction, copy or transmission
of this publication may be made without written permission.
No paragraph of this publication may be reproduced, copied
or transmitted save with written permission or in accordance
with the provisions of the Copyright Act 1956 (as amended).
Any person who does any unauthorised act in relation to this
publication may be liable to criminal prosecution and civil
claims for damages.

First published 1990 by Andersen Press Ltd

Picturemac edition published 1991 by
MACMILLAN CHILDREN'S BOOKS
A division of Macmillan Publishers Limited
London and Basingstoke
Associated companies throughout the world

ISBN 0-333-53785-8

A CIP catalogue record for this book is available
from the British Library

Printed in Hong Kong

Why Can't I Fly?

Ken Brown

M

MACMILLAN CHILDREN'S BOOKS

Early one morning, all the animals were gathered, as usual, by the water.
"I wish I could fly," thought the Ostrich. "Why can't I fly?" he asked the Sparrow.

"Maybe your neck is too long," suggested the Sparrow.
"The flamingoes have long necks and they can fly,"
replied the Ostrich, "so why can't I?"

"I don't know," chirped the Sparrow, "perhaps your legs
are too long."
"The storks have long legs and they can fly," said the
Ostrich, "so why can't I?"

"Well perhaps your wings are too small," said the Sparrow.
"You've got small wings and you can fly," answered the
Ostrich, "so why can't I?"
"Well, I don't know! Maybe you just don't try hard
enough," and so saying the Sparrow flew away.

"Try hard enough indeed!"
thought the Ostrich. "I'll show him.

I'll show all of them that I can fly."

So he ran as fast as he could

and, flapping his wings, he jumped off a high sand dune…

only to land, seconds later, with a terrible thud.

Next he climbed to the top of a huge rock.
"I'll show them!" he panted.
With his wings flailing the air, he threw himself over
the edge, but instantly plunged downwards and landed
headfirst in the soft sand below.

He remained with his head in the sand, too
embarrassed to show his face.
"I'll show them!" he thought." If my wings are too
small, I'll make them bigger."
Using some large leaves, bamboo canes, strong vines
and a great deal of skill, he constructed a flying machine.

Then he climbed to the top of the high rock again, and launched himself into the air.
"This is it! Look at me, everyone. I'm flying," cried the Ostrich.

But he spoke too soon! Moments later he landed with an almighty splash right in the middle of the river. "Never mind," said the Sparrow. "Your long neck will keep your head well above water!"

But the Ostrich was not put off by this, his first disastrous attempt at flying. He built another flying machine with even bigger wings and once again launched himself into the air.

"Out of my way!" he shouted to the doves. "Out of my way – I'm flying!"

Alas, this flight also ended in complete disaster, when the Ostrich became totally entangled in the leaves of a high palm tree.

"Never mind!" chirped the Sparrow. "Your long legs will certainly help you to get down from there."

The Ostrich, however, was just as determined as ever to fly; he would not give up. So he built an even bigger flying machine and for the third time climbed to the top of the high rock. He took a deep breath and launched himself yet again into the air. This time, instead of plummeting straight downwards as before, he soared high up into the sky, as gracefully as any other bird. "Look at me!" shouted the triumphant Ostrich. "Look, everybody, I'm flying!" But the only reply that he got was the sound of his own voice echoing about the empty skies.

The Ostrich couldn't understand it!

"Where is everyone?" he cried. "Where's Sparrow? I'm flying and there's no one here to see. They'll never believe me now."

But they did!

Other Picturemacs you will enjoy

BRINGING THE RAIN TO KAPITI PLAIN Verna Aardema
THUMBELINA Hans Christian Andersen/Susan Jeffers
BUSH VARK'S FIRST DAY OUT Charles Fuge
THE VILLAGE OF ROUND AND SQUARE HOUSES Ann Grifalconi
POOKINS GETS HER WAY Helen Lester/Lynn Munsinger
THERE'S SOMETHING SPOOKY IN MY ATTIC Mercer Mayer
HETTY AND HARRIET Graham Oakley
DIARY OF A CHURCH MOUSE Graham Oakley
HENRIETTA GOOSE Abigail Pizer
ALISTAIR UNDERWATER Marilyn Sadler/Roger Bollen
THE FLYAWAY PANTALOONS Sue Scullard
PENELOPE AND THE PIRATES James Young

For a complete list of Picturemac titles write to

Macmillan Children's Books
18–21 Cavaye Place, London SW10 9PG